Home

guide 2024

An adventurer pocket guidebook to exploring the

Fishing Capital of the World

ADELINE M. CREEL

TABLE OF CONTENT

Introduction

Homer, Alaska, sits on the beaches of Kachemak Bay and serves as a beacon of adventure, a cultural hub, and a refuge of stunning natural beauty. This picturesque town, known as the "Halibut Fishing Capital of the World," provides more than just a portal to extraordinary marine adventures; it invites you to a lifestyle woven with the threads of the great outdoors, artistic expressions, and society strongly connected to its surroundings.

Homer's geographical setting is nothing short of stunning. Perched on the edge of the Kenai Peninsula, it extends into the azure seas of Kachemak Bay, surrounded by rocky mountains and magnificent glaciers. The unusual location offers not only breathtaking views but also a playground for nature lovers and adventurers alike. Whether casting a line into the rich waters, strolling through lush trails, or taking the ideal shot of a bald eagle in flight, Homer provides a true Alaskan experience that begins at the end of the road and extends into the wilderness.

Homer's history is as colorful as the scenery around him. Originally inhabited by the Sugpiaq people, an Alutiiq group of Alaska Natives, the area has seen a variety of impacts. From Russian fur traders in the 1800s to homesteaders in the 1940s, each wave of migrants left a lasting imprint on the town's cultural landscape.

Today, Homer is known not only for its outdoor activities but also for its thriving artists community. The town is brimming with galleries, theatres, and artist studios, all of which reflect the area's vibrant creative energy. Annual events like the Homer Halibut Festival and the Kachemak Bay Writers' Conference attract tourists from all around, bringing the community and its guests together to celebrate the region's rich history and cultural energy.

One of Homer's most distinguishing characteristics is its dedication to environmental protection. The community recognizes the importance of its exceptional natural treasures and works relentlessly to preserve them. This mindset is visible everywhere, from the well-kept trails in Kachemak Bay State Park to locally-owned companies that prioritize sustainability. The Centre for Alaskan Coastal Studies, for example, is a community staple, providing educational programs and chances for visitors to participate in conservation efforts firsthand. This strong appreciation for nature not only protects the ecosystem but also improves the visitor experience, serving as a model for responsible tourism.

Regardless matter when you visit, Homer's calendar is packed with activities. Summer provides unlimited daylight, ideal for fishing trips, bear sightings across the water, and kayaking with sea otters. The autumn season brings brilliant foliage and a quieter time to explore the town's artistic treasures or go on a peaceful walk. Winter transforms the environment into a snowy wonderland, perfect for cross-country skiing, snowshoeing, and viewing the stunning northern lights. As spring arrives, the town awakens with migrating birds filling the skies, and the people rejoice in the return of longer days and warmer weather.

Homer's food scene is a wonderful reflection of its surroundings. Local eateries serve cuisine made with the freshest ingredients from the sea and land. Halibut and salmon are must-tries, typically caught on the same day they are served. The farmer's markets are overflowing with local vegetables, allowing every meal an opportunity to sample the region's abundance. For those who want a hands-on experience, several local enterprises provide cooking classes and culinary excursions, letting you delve deeper into Alaska's flavors.

While many visitors use Homer as a jumping-off point for experiencing the rest of Alaska, many discover that this town is a destination in and of itself. With its natural beauty, rich culture, and friendly residents, Homer provides a greater understanding of what it means to live in peace with the environment. Whether you are looking for isolation in the forest, the thrill of an outdoor adventure, or a calm retreat full of artistic inspiration, Homer welcomes you with open arms and offers an experience that will last long after you leave.

As you arrange your trip, let yourself be swept into the flow of life here. Engage with the locals, participate in the rituals, and allow the spirit of Homer to influence your perception of what a journey may be. Welcome to Homer, where every visit is an adventure with a story.

Getting To Know Homer

Homer, Alaska, is located at the end of the Sterling Highway on the shores of Kachemak Bay and provides a pristine view of the region's immense environment and fascinating history. This section of your book digs into Homer's topographical complexity, historical narratives, and climatic conditions, providing critical information for tourists looking to fully immerse themselves in this unique region.

Geographic Overview

Homer's location on the Kenai Peninsula provides more than simply beautiful scenery; it is also a geological and ecological hotspot. The town is best notable for the Homer Spit, a 4.5-mile-long thin point of land that extends into the bay and is lined with shops, restaurants, and beaches on both sides. This natural feature is not only a commercial and recreational hub, but it also serves as a protective barrier for the harbor, demonstrating a combination of human effort and natural formation.

The surroundings around Homer are varied, promising adventure and discovery. To the east, the rocky Kenai Mountains rise steeply, providing excellent climbing, sightseeing, and shooting opportunities. Kachemak Bay State Park, located across the bay to the south and west, is a pristine wilderness of 400,000 acres that includes islands, mountains, glaciers, woods, and ocean. These natural landscapes provide habitat for a wide range of wildlife, including moose and bears, whales, and sea otters, making Homer a popular visit for nature aficionados.

A Brief History of Homer.

Homer's history is as complex as the coastal cliffs. The Sugpiaq, an indigenous Alaskan clan that took advantage of the area's abundant land and sea resources, were the first to settle there. The town's contemporary name is derived from Homer Pennock, a conman who created a gold mining base in 1896. Though the gold rushes were mainly fruitless, the community persevered, shifting from mine to coal, and then to fishing and canning.

Throughout the twentieth century, Homer's economy shifted from survival to one enriched by its natural riches and beauty, drawing artists, explorers, and others seeking to live close to nature. The 1964 Alaska earthquake caused a major impact by elevating the seabed and permanently altering the nearby landscape. Today, Homer's economy is based on tourism, fishing, and the arts, with a strong emphasis on sustainability and cultural respect, reflecting the town's historical transformation from a resource-dependent outpost to a modern refuge for creativity and environmental stewardship.

The Climate in Homer: Best Time to Visit

Understanding Homer's climate is essential for planning your visit, as the weather has a considerable impact on the kind of activities offered. The Pacific Ocean moderates the climate of Homer, making it comparatively temperate for Alaska. Summers are cool, with typical high temperatures in the mid-60s Fahrenheit (about 18°C), making them great for fishing, hiking, and wildlife viewing. Summer's long days allow for plenty of sunshine to explore the great outdoors and enjoy the midnight sun.

Spring and autumn are transitional seasons that provide unique chances for visitors. Spring brings a resurgence of life as flora and fauna emerge from the frigid winter, and migrating birds return to fill the air with music. The town is less crowded, allowing for a more personal connection with nature. Autumn, on the other hand, is distinguished by beautiful displays of autumn foliage, cooler temperatures, and the start of the aurora borealis viewing season, which lasts until the colder, clearer evenings of winter.

Winter in Homer is peaceful and gives a unique beauty. Snow blankets the countryside, transforming the town into a peaceful winter wonderland. This season is ideal for cross-country skiing, snowmobiling, and ice fishing. While temperatures may plummet, the maritime effect maintains winters milder than in the interior of Alaska. With fewer tourists, there are more possibilities to explore local culture and community events, which offer warmth to the chilly months.

Homer's charm and activities change with the seasons, making it a year-round visit. Whether you're drawn to the mountains, the sea, or the pull of history and culture, Homer offers a backdrop that varies not just with the seasons, but also with the shifting tides of its vibrant community and natural surroundings. As you plan for your vacation, think about what you want out of your Alaskan adventure—Homer is ready to provide an experience as dynamic as the scenery.

Planning Your Trip to Homer, Alaska.

Traveling to Homer, Alaska requires careful planning to ensure a smooth and pleasurable vacation. Understanding admission requirements and packing basics, as well as managing your money and obtaining suitable travel insurance, are all critical steps in creating a great vacation. This book offers you with detailed information to help you prepare for your journey to this unique part of the world.

Entry Requirements

Travelers to Homer should be aware of the entry procedures for Alaska, and by extension, the United States. Traveling to Homer is simple for US nationals; a state-issued driver's license or another type of government-issued ID is necessary for admission by plane or land. However, following the Real ID Act, it is recommended that your identity fulfill government criteria, particularly for aviation travel.

International travelers must have a valid passport and, for many countries, a visa or authorization through the Visa Waiver Program's Electronic System for Travel Authorization (ESTA).

It is critical to review the most recent requirements from the United States. Contact the Department of State or your local United States embassy or consulate well in advance of your intended trip. Furthermore, because of the shifting global health landscape, it is recommended that you check for any pandemic-related travel recommendations or requirements.

Travel Tips

Traveling to Homer provides a mix of outdoor adventure and small-town charm, but keep these practical tips in mind:

Best Time to Visit: Homer is delightful all year, but the ideal time to visit is determined by your interests. Summer activities include fishing, hiking, and wildlife viewing, whilst winter is ideal for aurora viewing and winter sports.

Local Transportation: Renting a car is strongly advised because it allows you to explore Homer and its surroundings at your own pace. While the town itself is walkable, many of the attractions are scattered throughout the area.

Staying Connected: Mobile service is accessible in Homer with strong coverage, but in more rural regions of the bay, service may be restricted or nonexistent. It is wise to plan for intermittent disconnectivity, especially while going on wilderness adventures.

Packing Essentials

Packing for Homer should consider the variety of activities you may partake in as well as the changeable weather conditions:

Clothing: Layering is essential. Include foundation and insulating layers, as well as a waterproof outer layer. Even in the summer, temperatures can vary, particularly near water or at higher elevations.

Footwear: Durable, waterproof hiking boots are required for exploring the routes and terrain. Comfortable walking shoes are ideal for strolls and exploring the town.

Gear: Depending on your activity, carry fishing gear, binoculars for bird viewing, additional batteries for cameras, and any specialized equipment you choose to use, such as kayaks or bicycles.

Miscellaneous: Remember to include sunglasses, sunscreen, bug repellant, a first-aid kit, and any prescriptions you may require.

Budgeting for Your Trip

Budgeting for your vacation to Homer can vary greatly depending on the type of experience you want. Consider the following categories.

Accommodation: Accommodation options include camping, RV parks, bed and breakfasts, and luxury lodges. Booking in advance can help you get better rates, especially during the busy tourist season in the summer.

Dining: Homer's culinary culture ranges from simple diners and food trucks to fancy restaurants serving local fish. Plan to eat fresh seafood, but also consider self-catering if your accommodations allow it.

Activities: Many outdoor activities, such as hiking or beachcombing, are free or inexpensive. However, guided tours, fishing charters, and nature cruises will increase your expenses. Search for bundle offers or group savings.

Miscellaneous Expenses: Leave room for unforeseen expenses such as souvenirs, extra activities, or emergency supplies.

Travel and Health Insurance

Obtaining travel and health insurance is critical, especially if your home country's health coverage does not extend to the United States. Look for coverage that covers medical emergencies, travel cancellations, missing luggage, and any special activities you intend to do, such as extreme sports. Make sure your policy's coverage limitations are appropriate for possible significant medical bills in the United States.

Consider adding medical evacuation insurance, especially given Homer's rural location, which may necessitate relocation to more comprehensive medical facilities in the event of a significant health condition. Always have evidence of insurance with you and know how to file a claim if necessary.

Preparing for your vacation to Homer with careful attention to these details will allow you to fully enjoy everything this magnificent destination has to offer without interruption. With proper planning, your trip to Homer may be nothing short of extraordinary, full of the beauty and adventure that only Alaska can offer.

Transportation to Homer, Alaska

Planning a trip to Homer, Alaska, entails determining the best means to arrive and experience this magnificent destination. Knowing your transportation options, whether you're flying into Alaska or driving through the breathtaking scenery, improves your overall trip experience. This guide will provide vital travel information, such as how to get to Homer and the best local transport alternatives once you arrive.

How To Get to Homer

Homer's remote position on Alaska's Kenai Peninsula makes the travel an experience. The following are the major routes to access this picturesque town:

By Air

Anchorage to Homer Direct Flights: Most travelers begin their journey at Ted Stevens Anchorage

International Airport, Alaska's largest hub. From Anchorage, take a direct trip to Homer Airport, which is served by various local carriers. These flights last around 45 minutes and provide breathtaking aerial views of the Alaskan wilderness.

Scenic Flights: Charter flights are available for those seeking a more beautiful route. These provide a beautiful view of the glaciers, mountains, and coastlines as you travel to Homer.

By Road

Driving from Anchorage: If you prefer to drive, the distance from Anchorage to Homer is around 220 miles and takes four to five hours. The drive along the Seward and Sterling Highways is known for its stunning beauty. You will go through mountains, along coasts, and near active volcanoes.

Car Rentals: Car rentals are offered at the Anchorage International Airport. Renting a car not only makes driving to Homer easier but also allows for convenient local mobility within the town and its surroundings.

By the Sea

Ferry Services: The Alaska Marine Highway System does not reach Homer directly, but you can take a ferry to adjacent areas such as Seward or Whittier and then drive or take a bus from there. This option adds a maritime touch to your trip, allowing you to see Alaska's marine ecosystem firsthand.

By bus:

Intercity Buses: For individuals who do not want to drive, bus transportation from Anchorage to Homer is provided. These buses provide a comfortable trip with Wi-Fi and other amenities, allowing you to unwind and enjoy the scenery while you travel.

Local Transportation: Getting Around Homer.

Once in Homer, there are numerous methods to get around the town and its attractions. The options range from auto rentals to local shuttle services, each with a unique speed and perspective of Homer.

Car Rental

Flexibility and Convenience: Renting a car is the most flexible way to explore Homer and the surrounding areas at your leisure. Several rental agencies are located at or near Homer Airport, allowing for fast access to a vehicle upon arrival.

Taxis and rideshares:

Taxi Services: Homer offers various taxi companies that may be easily contacted for brief trips around town or a planned day of sightseeing.

Ridesharing Services: While ridesharing services are more limited than in larger cities, they are nonetheless available and can be a practical choice for point-to-point travel within Homer.

Bike Rentals:

Eco-Friendly Exploration: Bike rentals are offered for individuals who wish to stay active. Biking is a great way to explore Homer Spit and other gorgeous sites at your leisure, it's a healthier and more environmentally responsible option than driving.

Public transport:

Homer Trolley: During the summer months, a tourist trolley travels a set route through Homer, stopping at important sights. This service is not only inexpensive, but it also provides a unique and charming approach to seeing the town.

Shuttle Services: Several local businesses provide shuttle services, which are especially beneficial for accessing hiking trails or distant regions of Kachemak Bay State Park where other modes of transportation are inconvenient.

Walking:

Pedestrian-Friendly Areas: Homer is notably pedestrian-friendly, particularly along the Homer Spit and the town center. Many of Homer's attractions are within walking distance of one another, making it a viable and fun activity.

Arriving in and visiting Homer can be as distinctive as the destination itself. Whether you choose the speed and efficiency of a flight, the picturesque beauty of a drive, or the thrill of sea travel, getting to Homer marks the start of your Alaskan journey. Once there, a variety of local transit alternatives allow each guest to personalize their trip to their speed and preferences. From the independence of a rental car to the quaint elegance of a tram, moving around Homer is an essential part of the experience, ensuring that every moment in Alaska is as captivating as the scenery.

Accommodations in Homer

Homer, Alaska, has a wide range of lodgings to satisfy all types of travelers. Whether you're looking for luxury accommodations with beautiful views, a cozy bed & breakfast, or a rustic cabin surrounded by nature, Homer has something for everyone. This guide will go over the greatest locations to stay, ensuring you find the ideal home away from home during your vacation.

Hotels & Inns

Land's End Resort: Located at the end of the Homer Spit, this resort offers breathtaking panoramic views of Kachemak Bay, the mountains, and glaciers. This resort has a variety of rooms, ranging from ordinary rooms to magnificent suites with their balconies. On-site amenities include a fine dining restaurant, spa, and direct beach access. Land's End is a popular choice for travelers wishing to relax and appreciate Homer's natural beauty because of its calm environment and excellent service.

Homer Inn & Spa: For a more private and upmarket experience, the Homer Inn & Spa provides boutique rooms that prioritize relaxation and wellness. Each room is tastefully decorated and furnished with modern facilities. The on-site spa provides a variety of treatments, including massages and facials, ideal for resting after a day of exploration. The inn's location allows for easy access to the beach and beautiful views of the sea.

Best Western Bidarka Inn: The Best Western Bidarka Inn, conveniently located near downtown Homer, is an excellent choice for travelers seeking comfort and convenience. The hotel has spacious rooms with modern conveniences, such as free Wi-Fi and breakfast. Guests can also make use of the on-site fitness center and restaurant. Its central position makes it convenient to visit nearby attractions, shops, and restaurants.

Bed & Breakfasts

Juneberry Lodge: Nestled in a tranquil position with magnificent views of the mountains and bay,

Juneberry Lodge provides a warm and welcoming environment. This beautiful bed & breakfast offers cozy rooms with rustic decor, private toilets, and a full homemade breakfast provided every day. The hosts are well-known for their warmth and local knowledge, and they regularly provide guests with helpful suggestions and recommendations.

The Spyglass Inn: Located near downtown Homer, the Spyglass Inn provides a cozy and comfortable hotel with personalized service. Each room is carefully furnished to reflect Homer's charm and character. Guests can enjoy a tasty breakfast prepared using locally sourced products. The inn's central position provides easy access to nearby shops, galleries, and restaurants.

Alaska's Ridgewood Wilderness Lodge: Ridgewood Wilderness Lodge in Alaska offers a one-of-a-kind bed and breakfast experience. Located across Kachemak Bay, this resort provides an immersive Alaskan trip with excellent rooms. Visitors can enjoy guided treks, animal watching, and delicious lunches.

The lodge's distant position offers a tranquil refuge ideal for nature enthusiasts.

Cabins & Cottages

Baycrest Lodge: With luxury cottages and breathtaking views of Kachemak Bay, Baycrest Lodge offers the ideal combination of comfort and nature. Each cottage features modern conveniences such as full kitchens, private hot tubs, and outdoor decks. The tranquil atmosphere and breathtaking views make it an excellent alternative for anyone looking for a more private and quiet vacation.

Kenai Peninsula Suites: These distinctive, eco-friendly accommodations are perched on a bluff overlooking Cook Inlet. Kenai Peninsula Suites provides a choice of lodgings, ranging from cozy cabins to bigger suites, all designed with sustainability in mind. Each unit has modern conveniences, a private outdoor space, and access to a communal fire pit and grill area. The location provides convenient access to hiking trails and local animal viewing.

Homer Seaside Cottages: Located near the beach and downtown Homer, these beautiful cottages make an ideal base for exploring the area. Each cottage is completely furnished and includes a kitchen, making it perfect for families or extended visits. The warm hosts and welcoming atmosphere make for a delightful and memorable experience.

Campgrounds and RV parks

Homer Spit Campground: For those who prefer camping, the Homer Spit Campground is at an ideal location right on the shore. The campsite offers tent sites, RV sites with full hookups, and basic facilities like restrooms and showers. Waking up to the sound of the waves and the sight of the mountains is a memorable experience. Its proximity to the harbor and local stores makes it an ideal choice for campers.

Ocean Shores RV Park: Located near the heart of Homer, Ocean Shores RV Park provides a comfortable and scenic setting for your RV. The park offers spacious sites with full hookups, clean restrooms, and laundry facilities. Guests have direct access to the beach and stunning views of the bay. The central location allows you to easily explore Homer's attractions and activities.

Kachemak Bay State Park: Kachemak Bay State Park's campgrounds offer a more rustic and adventurous camping experience. These water taxi-accessible sites provide a true wilderness experience with minimal facilities. Campers can enjoy the stunning natural surroundings, hiking trails, and opportunities to see wildlife. This option is ideal for those who want to immerse themselves in nature.

Vacation Rentals

VRBO and Airbnb: Homer offers a wide range of vacation rentals through platforms such as VRBO and Airbnb. These rentals range from cozy cabins and beachfront cottages to large homes with modern amenities. Vacation rentals offer the convenience of self-catering and the comfort of a home-like setting. Whether you're traveling with family, friends, or as a couple, you can find a rental that meets your requirements and budget.

Homer Hideaway: The Homer Hideaway offers a one-of-a-kind vacation rental experience. This secluded property provides a range of accommodations, including a rustic cabin and a modern guesthouse. Each unit is deliberately constructed for comfort and convenience, with breathtaking views of the surrounding nature. The serene surroundings and personalized touches make it an ideal hideaway.

Unique Stays

Halibut Cove Experience: Just across Kachemak Bay, Halibut Cove offers a special Alaskan experience. Accessible only by boat, this little hamlet has unusual hotels such as lakeside bungalows and quaint inns. Staying in Halibut Cove allows you to experience the peace and beauty of this remote area, with options for kayaking, hiking, and dining at the acclaimed Saltry Restaurant.

Yurt Stays: For a truly unique and immersive experience, consider staying in a yurt. Several locales surrounding Homer offer yurt accommodations, giving a blend of rural beauty and modern comfort. Yurts are normally outfitted with comfy beds, heating, and rudimentary kitchen facilities. The circular form and skylight allow for a pleasant and personal connection with the natural environment.

Homer's broad choice of accommodations guarantees that any visitor can find the appropriate place to stay, whether you're seeking luxury, adventure, or a comfortable getaway. From seaside resorts and lovely bed & breakfasts to rustic cabins and distinctive yurts, each lodging option offers its own unique experience, boosting your visit to this captivating Alaskan town. Whatever your preferences, you're likely to find a welcome and comfortable base from which to enjoy the natural beauty and rich culture of Homer, Alaska.

Travel Tips and Safety Information for Homer, Alaska

Traveling to Homer, Alaska promises a unique and memorable experience filled with stunning landscapes, fascinating cultural experiences, and a wide selection of outdoor activities. To ensure your trip is as pleasurable and secure as possible, it's crucial to be well-prepared. This book contains critical travel recommendations and safety information to help you make the most of your visit to Homer.

Preparing for Your Trip

Research and Plan Ahead: Before leaving, spend some time researching Homer and its attractions. Make a flexible itinerary with must-see attractions, activities, and food alternatives. Booking lodgings and tours ahead of time, especially during high season, will help you obtain your chosen selections while avoiding last-minute headaches.

Travel Insurance: Travel insurance is a sensible investment. It can cover unforeseen circumstances like vacation cancellations, medical emergencies, and misplaced luggage. Ensure that your coverage includes medical evacuation, especially since Homer is in a remote region and accessing extensive medical services may necessitate transportation to Anchorage or other major cities.

Health Precautions: If you have any medical conditions, speak with your doctor before traveling. Bring an adequate supply of any prescription medications, as access to pharmacies may be limited. Carry a basic first-aid kit that includes bandages, antiseptic, pain medicines, and any personal health supplies.

Documents: Make sure you have the appropriate travel documents, such as a valid ID or passport. Make copies of all critical documents, including your driver's license, passport, and insurance policy. Keep these copies apart from the originals, and think about storing digital copies in a secure cloud service.

Packing Smart

Clothing: The weather in Homer can be unpredictable, so bring layers. Use a combination of base layers, insulating layers, and a waterproof outer layer. Even in July, temperatures might dip in the evenings, so bring warm clothes. Remember to include a decent pair of waterproof hiking boots, a hat, gloves, and a scarf.

Gear and Accessories: Depending on your planned activities, you may require specialized equipment. Binoculars for bird observation, a camera with additional batteries, and fishing equipment can all improve your experience. Don't forget your sunglasses, sunscreen, insect repellent, and reusable water bottle.

Electronics and Connectivity: Although Homer has adequate mobile coverage, certain outlying spots may not. Bring a portable charger for your electronics, especially if you plan to go trekking or spend long periods outside. A GPS gadget can help you navigate in places with poor cell service.

Safety in the wilderness.

species Awareness: Homer is home to a variety of species, including bears, moose, and marine mammals. Learn about wildlife safety guidelines. To avoid attracting animals, keep a safe distance away from them, never feed them, and store food and rubbish properly. If you go trekking, bring bear spray and know how to use it.

Hiking Safety: Always inform someone about your plans before embarking on a walk. Stay on marked routes and avoid hiking alone. Bring a map, a compass, and enough supplies, such as water, food, and a first aid kit. Prepare for unexpected weather changes by packing appropriate clothing and supplies.

Water Safety: The waters surrounding Homer can be cold and choppy. If you intend to kayak, fish, or participate in other water sports, always wear a life jacket. Check the weather and tidal forecasts before leaving, and be mindful of potential hazards such as strong currents and rapid weather changes.

Navigating the Town

Local Transportation: Renting a car is advised for exploring Homer and the nearby area. Drive carefully, particularly in unknown or difficult terrain. If you're walking or biking, stick to specified trails and be careful of traffic. Those who rely on public transportation should check timetables in advance, since services may be limited.

Emergency Services: Learn about the locations of local emergency services, such as the hospital, police station, and fire department. In case of an emergency, call 911. It is also beneficial to know the contact information for your country's embassy or consulate.

Personal Safety: Homer is normally safe, although it is always advisable to take standard precautions. Keep your items safe, don't leave valuables in your car, and stay attentive to your surroundings, especially at night. Trust your intuition and don't be afraid to contact locals or authorities for assistance if necessary.

Respecting the Local Culture and Environment

Cultural Sensitivity: Show respect for local customs and traditions. Engage with the community nicely and respectfully. Learn a few basic phrases in the local language, such as greetings and thank yous, to demonstrate your gratitude and respect.

Environmental Responsibility: Homer's natural beauty is one of its most valuable assets. Help maintain it by adhering to Leave No Trace principles. Dispose of waste appropriately, stick to authorized pathways, and avoid disturbing wildlife. Support local conservation initiatives and, whenever possible, select eco-friendly tours and activities.

Practical Tips

Local Cuisine: Don't miss out on sampling local dishes. Homer is known for its fresh fish, especially halibut and salmon. Local farmers' markets offer fresh vegetables and artisanal products. Dining at local eateries not only provides a taste of the location but also benefits the local economy.

Budgeting: While Homer has a variety of lodging and food alternatives, the expenditures can rapidly mount up. Create a budget that covers accommodations, meals, activities, transportation, and a contingency fund for unexpected expenses. Search for package packages or discounts on tours and activities.

Connectivity & Communication: While Homer has strong cellphone service, it's always a good idea to alert someone about your plans, especially if you're going to a distant location. Many hotels and cafes provide free Wi-Fi, but a mobile data package is useful for navigation and emergency communication.

By planning ahead of time and keeping these travel tips and safety information in mind, you can have a safe, enjoyable, and enriching vacation in Homer, Alaska. This magnificent town has a multitude of natural beauties, cultural events, and outdoor excursions that are best enjoyed with little planning and consideration. Whether you're hiking the gorgeous trails, exploring the diverse marine life, or simply admiring the breathtaking vistas, Homer guarantees a memorable adventure that will leave you with lasting memories.

Homer Spit, Gateway to Kachemak Bay

The Homer Spit is one of Alaska's most famous and distinctive geographical features, combining natural beauty, recreational activities, and a thriving local culture. This short strip of land, which extends 4.5 miles into the waters of Kachemak Bay, is a center of activity and a must-see location for anybody visiting Homer. Here's an in-depth look at what makes Homer Spit such an outstanding gateway to Kachemak Bay.

The Homer Spit formed as a result of geological processes that occurred over thousands of years. Glaciers, ocean currents, and sediment deposition shaped this natural sandbar into the long, slender peninsula that we see today. Historically, indigenous peoples relied on the Spit for fishing and trading. As settlers arrived, it grew into a thriving port and commercial fishing hub, which remains a pillar of Homer's economy.

Activities and Attractions at the Spit

The Small Boat Harbor: The Small Boat Harbour is located in the heart of the Homer Spit and serves as a busy port for fishing boats, yachts, and water taxis. Visitors can stroll along the docks, watching fishermen and boaters go about their daily activities, or embark on their maritime adventure. Many of Homer's sea excursions, such as fishing charters, wildlife tours, and trips across Kachemak Bay, begin at the harbor.

Fishing: Known as the "Halibut Fishing Capital of the World," the Spit provides unparalleled opportunities for anglers. Fishing charters operate every day and offer trips ranging from half-day to multi-day durations. Whether you're a seasoned angler or a beginner, the knowledgeable guides can help you catch a prize halibut, salmon, or rockfish. For those who prefer a more leisurely experience, fishing off the end of the Spit is a popular and profitable pastime.

Beaches and Tide Pools: The Spit's beaches are ideal for a wide range of activities. The calm bay waters are ideal for beachcombing and exploring tide pools teeming with marine life. The ocean side features a more rugged coastline with crashing waves and dramatic views. Visitors can spend hours strolling along the beach, collecting shells and admiring the ever-changing scenery.

The Seafarer's Memorial: A poignant landmark on the Spit is the Seafarer's Memorial, which honors those who died at sea. This touching tribute includes a memorial wall and a sculpture of a sailor looking out to sea, reminding visitors of the powerful bond between the community and the ocean. It's a place for reflection and a reminder of the risks and rewards of life by the sea.

Salty Dawg Saloon: No visit to the Spit would be complete without a stop at the iconic Salty Dawg Saloon. Originally a lighthouse, this historic building has been serving drinks since 1957 and is a favorite haunt of locals and tourists alike. The interior is decorated with thousands of dollar bills signed by visitors, creating a unique and lively atmosphere. It's a great spot to unwind with a drink and soak in the local flavor.

Art and Culture

Homer Spit Artists: The creative spirit of Homer is alive and well on the Spit. Numerous galleries and shops showcase the works of local artists, offering everything from paintings and sculptures to handmade jewelry and crafts. Visitors can meet the artists, learn about their techniques, and purchase unique pieces that capture the essence of Alaska.

Annual Events: The Homer Spit is also the venue for various events throughout the year, adding to its vibrant atmosphere. Highlights include the annual Homer Halibut Derby, where anglers compete for the biggest catch, and the Kachemak Bay Shorebird Festival, which celebrates the return of migratory birds each spring with guided bird walks, workshops, and presentations.

Dining and Shopping

Seafood Delights: The culinary scene on the Spit is heavily influenced by its maritime heritage. Fresh seafood is the star of the show, with many restaurants offering daily catches prepared in various delectable ways. From casual fish and chips to gourmet dining experiences, the flavors of the ocean are expertly showcased.

Local Eateries: In addition to seafood, visitors can enjoy a variety of other dining options. Cozy cafes, food trucks, and waterfront bistros serve everything from hearty breakfasts to sumptuous dinners. Many establishments boast stunning views of the bay, making dining a memorable experience.

Unique Shops: The Spit is home to a range of shops and boutiques that offer an eclectic mix of goods. Visitors can find Alaskan-made souvenirs, outdoor gear, and artisanal products. Whether you're looking for a memento for your trip or practical items for your adventures, the shops on the Spit have something for everyone.

Wildlife Viewing

Marine Life: Kachemak Bay's rich marine environment is home to a diverse array of wildlife. From the Spit, visitors can observe sea otters playing in the kelp beds, harbor seals lounging on the rocks, and occasionally, the majestic spout of a passing whale. Wildlife tours and cruises enable closer experiences with these aquatic dwellers, providing insights into their activities and habitats.

Bird Watching: The Homer Spit is a birdwatcher's paradise, especially during the spring and fall migrations. The huge mudflats and estuaries attract hundreds of shorebirds, ducks, and raptors. Birders can spot animals like the sandhill crane, bald eagle, and numerous varieties of gulls and ducks. The Kachemak Bay Shorebird Festival is a highlight for birding aficionados, including guided excursions and informative events.

Outdoor Adventures

Kayaking & Paddleboarding: The tranquil waters near the Spit are great for kayaking and paddleboarding. Rentals and guided tours are offered for all skill levels, providing a unique perspective of the bay's natural splendor. Paddlers can explore hidden coves, witness wildlife up close, and enjoy the tranquil setting.

Hiking and Biking: While the Spit itself is quite level, the surrounding surroundings offer good chances for hiking and biking. Trails at Kachemak Bay State Park and adjacent places allow access to spectacular panoramas, lush forests, and alpine meadows. Whether you prefer a leisurely walk or a difficult hike, the region has lots to offer.

Camping: For those who love the outdoors, camping on the Spit is a popular alternative. Campgrounds offer spaces for tents and RVs, allowing tourists to camp right on the beach and fall asleep to the sound of the waves. It's a terrific way to immerse oneself in the natural beauty of the area.

The Homer Spit is more than just a geographical feature; it's the heart of Homer's community and a gateway to the wonders of Kachemak Bay. Its blend of natural beauty, cultural depth, and recreational activities make it an essential destination for anybody visiting Homer. Whether you're fishing, discovering tidal pools, feasting on fresh seafood, or simply admiring the scenery, the Spit provides an amazing experience that encapsulates Alaska's coastal beauty.

Pratt Museum: A Window to Homer's History

The Pratt Museum, located in the heart of Homer, Alaska, is a cultural landmark that provides visitors with an in-depth understanding of the region's history, art, and ecology.

This local treasure not only highlights the area's unique heritage, but also functions as a thriving community center, attracting both locals and tourists with interactive exhibits, educational programs, and conservation activities. Exploring the Pratt Museum is like going through a gateway into Homer's past and future, showcasing the environmental and human tales that form this region of Alaska.

The Pratt Museum was founded in 1967 by a group of visionary community people who recognized the value of conserving Kachemak Bay's rich history and unique ecosystems. The museum, named for Sam Pratt, a local champion in education and conservation, has evolved from a small collection in a log cabin to a modern facility focused on education, culture, and environmental care.

The museum's purpose is to provide better knowledge and respect for the area's historical, artistic, and ecological value. The Pratt Museum's exhibits and programs not only preserve local history but also motivate visitors to interact with and safeguard the natural world around them.

Architectural Design and Setting

The architecture of the Pratt Museum reflects its environmental and cultural goals. The structure was designed to blend in with its environment, with natural materials and huge windows that provide panoramic views of the surrounding mountains and Kachemak Bay. The museum is surrounded by beautifully maintained grounds, featuring a native plant garden that serves as a habitat for local species while also providing visitors with a tranquil environment to explore.

Permanent Exhibitions and Collections

The Seldovia Village Tribe's Basketry Collection:
One of the museum's most treasured exhibits is a stunning collection of traditional basketry. These items, created by the indigenous Dena'ina and Sugpiaq peoples, are not only exquisite works of art but also examples of complicated weaving skills passed down through centuries.

Maritime History Gallery: This exhibit explores Homer's historical link with the sea. It displays fishing-related artifacts, models of fishing boats, and archive images documenting the growth of nautical activity in the area. Visitors can listen to stories from old fishermen and learn about the hardships and accomplishments of life on the water through interactive displays.

Homesteading in Alaska: This exhibit brings viewers back to a time when brave souls trekked into the Alaskan wilderness to claim property and start new lives. The display includes tools, diaries, photographs, and personal objects that illustrate the lives of these homesteaders while emphasizing their tenacity and inventiveness.

Ecology of Kachemak Bay: The Ecology of Kachemak Bay is a dynamic exhibit that highlights the bay's different ecosystems and neighboring places. It features interactive maps, multimedia displays, and specimens that demonstrate the intricate interdependence of the region's vegetation and fauna.

Temporary Exhibitions and Art Installations

The Pratt Museum also showcases rotating exhibits on current issues, local artists, and temporary presentations from other institutions. These shows are intended to engage the community and spark a discussion about current events, artistic expression, and environmental challenges. For example, an exhibit on climate change in the Arctic may include local scientific findings, interactive models, and artwork influenced by environmental themes.

Education Programs and Community Engagement

Educational seminars: The museum provides seminars for people of all ages on a wide range of topics, including art, culture, science, and nature. These workshops are frequently taught by specialists and local craftspeople, who provide hands-on learning opportunities that are both educational and enjoyable.

Community Events: The Pratt Museum hosts lectures, film screenings, and cultural festivities. These gatherings promote a sense of community and give a forum for sharing information and experiences.

School Partnerships: The museum collaborates closely with local schools to offer educational programs that supplement classroom instruction. Field trips to museums are a highlight for many kids, allowing them to interact with their cultural and natural heritage in a dynamic atmosphere.

Conservation efforts

The Pratt Museum actively participates in local conservation efforts, using its exhibits and resources to raise environmental awareness and action. The museum works with local environmental organizations, research institutions, and government agencies to fund projects that protect the region's natural resources.

Kachemak Bay State Park: Adventures in Nature

Kachemak Bay State Park, located on the southern edge of Alaska's Kenai Peninsula, is home to a diverse range of ecosystems, including glacial valleys, rugged coastlines, dense forests, and alpine meadows. As Alaska's first state park, it spans over 400,000 acres of pristine wilderness, offering limitless opportunities for adventure and discovery. This guide delves deeply into the wonders of Kachemak Bay State Park, emphasizing its natural beauty, diverse wildlife, and variety of outdoor activities.

Kachemak Bay State Park, which opened in 1970, has captured the hearts of nature enthusiasts with its breathtaking landscapes and diverse wildlife. The park's remote location, accessible only by boat or floatplane from Homer, adds to its allure, providing a true escape into nature. This vast area contains a mix of ocean, ice, forest, and mountain environments, each supporting a unique flora and fauna that contributes to the region's ecological diversity.

Geographical Features.

The environment: The park's environment is a breathtaking display of nature's handiwork, with jagged coastlines, beautiful peaks, and tranquil beaches. The natural forces of glaciers and ocean tides sculpt the dynamic environment, making it both tough and rewarding to explore.

Glaciers and Ice Fields: The park contains multiple glaciers, including the Grewingk Glacier, which is a famous tourist attraction. These icy giants are tremendous change agents, sculpting the landscape and forming natural phenomena such as moraines and kettle ponds.

Forests and Meadows: Beyond the ice and rock, the park features rich forests of Sitka spruce and birch, intermingled with colorful alpine meadows that bloom with wildflowers throughout the spring and summer months. These landscapes provide not just a visual feast but also a habitat for various fauna.

Plants and Animals

Marine Life: The coastal waters of Kachemak Bay are rich in marine life, including sea otters, seals, and several fish species. The intertidal zones offer a view into the undersea world with tide pools filled with starfish, crabs, and anemones.

Terrestrial Wildlife: The park is a sanctuary for terrestrial wildlife, with animals such as moose, black bears, and mountain goats regularly spotted. The woodlands and meadows are also home to a plethora of bird species, including bald eagles, puffins, and sandhill cranes, making it a birdwatcher's delight.

Botanical Diversity: The varying climates and topographies within the park support a rich diversity of plant species. From the coastal sedge meadows to the subalpine flower fields, botany aficionados will find much to enjoy and study.

Recreational Opportunities

Hiking and Backpacking: Kachemak Bay State Park is a hiker's paradise, featuring paths that cater to all ability levels. From the easy stroll along the shore of Halibut Cove to the strenuous Alpine Ridge Trail that gives panoramic views of the bay and neighboring mountains, there is something for everyone.

Kayaking & Paddle Sports: Kachemak Bay's protected waters are suitable for kayaking and other paddle sports. Visitors can glide past coastal cliffs, visit secluded coves, or even head to distant beaches for a night beneath the stars.

Fishing and Hunting: The park's waterways are abundant in halibut, salmon, and other fish, making it a popular fishing destination. Hunting for black bears and waterfowl is permitted in certain regions during certain seasons, subject to tight laws to guarantee sustainable practices.

Camping: With so many campsites distributed around the park, camping is an excellent opportunity to immerse yourself in nature. Whether you choose a site near the beach or in the forest, camping at Kachemak Bay State Park is an unforgettable experience.

Conservation & Education

Preserving Wilderness: Conservation is an important part of the park's goal. Efforts are aimed at maintaining the natural environment while allowing people to learn and appreciate it. Visitors are asked to follow the Leave No Trace principles to reduce their impact on vulnerable ecosystems.

Educational programs: The park provides a variety of educational programs to teach visitors about the surrounding ecosystems, wildlife, and conservation initiatives. These programs are intended to create a greater respect and understanding of the natural world, as well as the need for environmental protection.

Visitor Tips

Planning Your Visit: Because the park is only accessible by boat or plane, you must arrange your visit in advance. Before you leave, check the weather forecast, tidal charts, and park cautions. Hiring a native guide can improve your trip, especially if you're inexperienced with the Alaskan environment.

Safety Precautions: Prepare for changing weather conditions by wearing layers and bringing waterproof gear. Be animal vigilant, carry bear spray, and understand how to safely store food. Navigating the area necessitates caution and consideration for natural hazards such as fast rivers and steep trails.

Kachemak Bay State Park provides a meaningful connection to nature through its breathtaking vistas, diversified ecosystems, and a plethora of recreational opportunities. Whether you're looking for solitude, adventure, or a chance to learn about the natural world, this park offers an unequaled opportunity to experience Alaska's raw splendor. By visiting Kachemak Bay State Park, you not only enter a world of adventure but also become a part of the park's continuing conservation and discovery story.

Carl Wynn Nature Centre: Exploring the Local Wildlife

The Carl Wynn Nature Centre, located just outside of the scenic town of Homer, Alaska, provides visitors with a unique opportunity to immerse themselves in the Kenai Peninsula's vast biodiversity. This 140-acre nature reserve, operated by the Centre for Alaskan Coastal Studies, serves as an important educational and environmental resource.

The center is committed to protecting natural habitats and educating the public about local flora and wildlife through interactive learning activities and guided tours. This in-depth examination will look at the Carl Wynn Nature Center's features, activities, and ecological significance.

The nature center was founded in the late twentieth century as a tribute to Carl Wynn, a passionate naturalist, and conservationist, and has since grown into a beloved community resource and a must-see destination for nature lovers. The center's location on the bluffs overlooking Kachemak Bay provides not only breathtaking views but also a unique ecological niche where maritime and terrestrial biomes collide, creating a diverse environment for a variety of species.

Natural features and habitats

The Carl Wynn Nature Centre has a variety of habitats, including dense spruce forests, vibrant meadows, peat bogs, and wetlands. This diversity stems from its geographic location between the coastal areas of Kachemak Bay and the higher, rougher terrains of the Kenai Mountains. Each habitat supports unique communities of plants and animals:

Spruce Forests: These forests, dominated by Sitka spruce, provide habitat and food for a variety of wildlife, including moose, snowshoe hares, and numerous bird species.

Meadows: In the summer, these areas bloom with wildflowers such as fireweed, lupine, and wild geranium, attracting pollinators like bees and butterflies.

Peat Bogs and Wetlands: These delicate ecosystems are essential for water filtration and carbon storage, and they are home to rare species like the carnivorous sundew plant.

Wildlife Observation and Conservation

The Carl Wynn Nature Centre is known for its abundance of wildlife. The center is critical to wildlife conservation by monitoring species and protecting habitat. Visitors can see a wide variety of fauna:

Mammals: Moose can often be seen grazing in the meadows. Smaller mammals like ermine, beavers, and red squirrels can also be spotted in various parts of the reserve.

Birds: The center is a haven for birdwatchers. It is home to bald eagles, sandhill cranes, and a variety of songbirds. The diverse habitats support both resident and migratory species, making it an excellent spot for seasonal bird observations.

Insects and Amphibians: The wetlands and meadows support a healthy population of insects, which in turn attract various amphibians. The center is an excellent place for studying the complex food webs and ecological interactions in these communities.

Educational Programs and Activities

The Carl Wynn Nature Center is committed to education and offers a variety of programs designed to engage visitors of all ages:

Guided Nature Walks: Experienced naturalists lead walks through the center's trails, providing insights into the local ecosystems and pointing out flora and fauna along the way.

Workshops and Lectures: Throughout the year, the center hosts workshops on topics ranging from wildlife photography to plant identification and ecological conservation strategies.

Youth Camps and School Programs: The center offers educational camps and programs for children, fostering an early appreciation for nature and teaching young people about the importance of environmental stewardship.

Trails and Hiking at the Center

The Carl Wynn Nature Center features several well-maintained trails that cater to various fitness levels and offer different perspectives of the area's natural beauty:

Meadow Loop Trail: An easy, flat trail that winds through wildflower meadows, ideal for families and those looking for a leisurely walk.

Forest Trail: A slightly more challenging route that takes visitors through dense spruce forests, offering opportunities to spot wildlife and learn about the local timber species.

Bluff Trail: For those seeking a more strenuous hike, this trail leads up to the bluffs overlooking

Kachemak Bay, offering breathtaking panoramic views.

Visitor Tips and Sustainability

To ensure a safe and enjoyable visit while maintaining the integrity of the ecosystems, visitors are encouraged to follow these guidelines:

Stay on Designated Trails: To protect plant life and minimize disturbance to wildlife, visitors should stick to marked trails.

No Littering: All trash should be packed out, and visitors should avoid leaving any trace of their visit.

Respect Wildlife: Observing animals from a distance, not feeding them, and being quiet and unobtrusive helps keep wildlife wild.

The Carl Wynn Nature Center is more than just a destination; it is an immersive experience that brings people closer to nature and fosters a deeper understanding of the importance of environmental preservation. Through its trails, educational programs, and dedicated conservation efforts, the center not only protects the natural beauty of Homer but also teaches visitors the value of coexistence with our natural surroundings. Whether you're an avid birdwatcher, a casual hiker, or someone with a passion for environment and conservation, the Carl Wynn Environment Center offers a gratifying and engaging experience that is guaranteed to inspire.

Activities and Adventures in Homer, Alaska

Homer, Alaska, is a paradise for outdoor enthusiasts, offering a huge assortment of activities that cater to all ages and experience levels. From the pleasure of fishing in the rich waters of Kachemak Bay to exploring gorgeous hiking routes, partaking in water sports, and seeing different bird species, Homer provides the perfect backdrop for adventure. This detailed guide delves into the greatest activities and adventures in the area, showcasing the best experiences for travelers wishing to connect with nature.

Fishing and Marine Life Tours

The Fishing Capital: Known as the "Halibut Fishing Capital of the World," Homer's waterways are packed with some of the best catch you can locate. Whether you're an expert angler or a newbie, the variety of fishing charters available allows everyone an opportunity to pull in a substantial catch. These charters give all the equipment and direction needed, and they're experts at navigating the local waters for the greatest fishing places.

Types of Fishing: In addition to halibut, fishermen can also target salmon, rockfish, and cod. Many charters provide multi-species trips, providing tourists with a thorough fishing experience. For those interested in fly fishing, the rivers and streams accessible by road or boat from Homer are good for capturing trout and salmon.

Marine Life Excursions: For non-fishing fans, marine life excursions are a fantastic alternative. These cruises offer near experiences with sea otters, seals, whales, and porpoises. Guided by professionals who provide comprehensive commentary on the ecosystem of Kachemak Bay, these experiences are both educational and enjoyable.

Hiking Trails: From Beginner to Advanced

A Trail for Every Trekker: Homer's trails range from short walks to strenuous hikes, appealing to all kinds of hikers. Each walk offers various landscapes and possibilities to encounter wildlife.

Beluga Slough walks: The Beluga Slough Trail is an easy, accessible walk ideal for families, with good birdwatching possibilities and breathtaking views of the bay.

Diamond Creek Walk: For those seeking more adventure, this walk leads through thick woodlands to a stunning beach. It's relatively difficult, but hikers are rewarded with seclusion and breathtaking ocean vistas.

Grace Ridge Trail: The Grace Ridge Trail is a challenging climb that advanced hikers will appreciate. This difficult walk to the ridge top provides stunning panoramic views of Kachemak Bay and the surrounding mountains.

Safety and Preparedness: Regardless of the terrain, it's critical to be prepared with the right gear, such as strong hiking boots, weather-appropriate clothing, water, food, and a basic first aid kit. Always tell someone about your trekking plans and planned return time.

Kayaking and Watersports

Kayaking the Bay: Kayaking is an excellent way to discover Kachemak Bay's secluded sections. Visitors can rent kayaks or participate in guided tours lasting from a few hours to several days. These tours frequently involve visits to remote beaches and coves that are not accessible by car.

Stand-Up Paddleboarding (SUP): For a more leisurely pace, stand-up paddleboarding is a pleasant way to enjoy the water while still getting a full-body workout. The tranquil seas around Homer Spit are ideal for beginners.

Water Safety: Always wear a life jacket while kayaking or participating in other water sports. Be mindful of the weather and water temperatures, and never go out alone without alerting someone of your plans.

Birdwatching Hotspots

A Birder's Haven: Homer is located on the Pacific Flyway, making it an ideal place for bird-watching. The area draws a diverse range of migratory and resident bird species, making it a year-round birding attraction.

Mud Bay: Mud Bay is a popular destination for migratory shorebirds throughout the spring and autumn seasons. Thousands of sandpipers, plovers, and other bird species can be seen during peak migration seasons.

Mariner Park Lagoon: This accessible area is ideal for observing ducks and wading birds. The lagoon's pathways and viewing platforms make it an ideal location for birders of all abilities.

Anchor River: This river not only provides excellent fishing opportunities but also draws a variety of bird species, including eagles and kingfishers.

Birding Ethics: When bird viewing, it is critical to respect the wildlife. Use binoculars for close-up views and avoid disturbing the birds, particularly during nesting season. Maintaining a respectful distance ensures that human presence does not interfere with the birds' normal behaviors.

Homer's diverse landscape provides an incredible variety of activities for outdoor enthusiasts. Whether you're casting a line into the deep sea, hiking through lush trails, paddling along tranquil waters, or admiring the magnificent array of avian species, Homer invites you to immerse yourself in its natural wonders. Each activity not only provides entertainment and adventure but also strengthens one's connection to Alaska's breathtaking natural surroundings.

Cultural Insights: Exploring the Art and Festivals of Homer, Alaska

Homer, Alaska, also known as the "cosmic hamlet by the sea," is well-known for its stunning natural landscapes and vibrant cultural scene. The town's artistic community, as well as its calendar of unique local festivals, provide visitors with an insight into its residents' creative and spirited lives. From galleries showcasing local art to events commemorating the region's heritage and natural bounty, Homer offers an enriching cultural experience to all who visit.

Local Art and Artists

Homer's Heartbeat: Art, like the sea and the sky, is an integral part of the environment. The town's artistic community is diverse, encompassing painting, sculpture, ceramics, and photography. Local artists frequently draw inspiration from the Kenai Peninsula's breathtaking natural beauty and wildlife, which is reflected in their work.

Gallery and Studio

Bunnell Street Arts Centre: The Bunnell Street Arts Centre is more than just a gallery; it is a cultural hub for Homer. It is a community arts organization that promotes local artists by hosting exhibitions, residencies, and workshops. The center exhibits innovative work, which frequently focuses on contemporary issues and indigenous art forms.

Ptarmigan Arts Gallery: Ptarmigan Arts Gallery is a cooperative gallery owned and operated by local artists. It showcases a diverse range of art forms, from traditional landscapes and wildlife portraits to abstract works and fine crafts. The gallery exemplifies the collaborative spirit of Homer's artistic community.

Fireweed Gallery: Known for its vibrant and eclectic collection, Fireweed Gallery represents many of Homer's most celebrated artists. The artwork here spans various styles and mediums, offering visitors a comprehensive view of the local art scene.

Artistic Events

Homer's First Friday: On the first Friday of each month, galleries, shops, and restaurants in Homer open their doors for an evening of art, music, and community. This event is a great opportunity for visitors to meet local artists, view new exhibitions, and experience the town's lively culture.

Artist-in-Residence Programs: Various local institutions, including the Bunnell Street Arts Center, offer artist-in-residence programs that attract both national and international artists. These programs encourage cultural exchange and provide artists with the opportunity to create work inspired by Homer's unique environment.

Festivals and Events

Homer's calendar is dotted with festivals and events that celebrate everything from the local cuisine to the arts and natural environment. These gatherings are not only fun and festive but also offer insights into the community's values and traditions.

Kachemak Bay Shorebird Festival: Held annually in early May, this is Alaska's largest wildlife festival. The event coincides with the peak migration of shorebirds, making it a fantastic period for birdwatching. The festival includes guided birding excursions, workshops, and presentations by wildlife experts.

Homer Halibut Festival: Celebrating Homer's title as the "Halibut Fishing Capital of the World," this festival occurs in June and features competitions, fresh seafood, music, and educational displays about marine conservation. It's a perfect blend of fun and learning, with activities that appeal to all ages.

Peony Celebration Day: Given Homer's perfect climate for growing peonies, this July festival celebrates the bloom season with garden tours, workshops, and a marketplace. The celebration showcases the beauty of Homer's peonies, which are sought after by florists and garden enthusiasts around the world.

Homer Highland Games: Taking place in August, the Homer Highland Games pay homage to Scottish culture with traditional music, dance, athletic activities, and plenty of kilts. This event is popular among locals and visitors alike, delivering a taste of Scotland in the heart of Alaska.

Nutcracker Faire: As the Christmas season approaches, the Nutcracker Faire in December brings the town together with a crafts market, live concerts, and the local production of "The Nutcracker Ballet." It's a delightful event that exhibits the artistic abilities and seasonal spirit of Homer.

Homer's cultural landscape is as diverse and vibrant as its natural surroundings. The town's artists and their creations give a window into the essence of this unique community, while its festivals and events bring to life the traditions and passions of its people. For visitors, connecting with Homer's art and participating in its cultural activities provide a greater knowledge of this Alaskan town, producing enduring memories of a place where nature and culture happily coexist.

Culinary Delights: A Taste of Homer

Homer, Alaska, is not simply a picturesque sanctuary located on the edge of Kachemak Bay; it's also a dynamic culinary hotspot that reflects the rich abundance of the sea and the ingenuity of its citizens. Homer's vibrant food scene, which includes everything from rustic seafood shacks to sophisticated restaurants, offers a diverse spectrum of flavors for both foodies and culinary adventurers. This in-depth examination looks into Homer's unique food culture, highlighting local specialties, dining experiences, and the individuals behind the culinary talent.

The Foundation of Homer's Culinary Scene

Homer's culinary landscape is deeply rooted in the natural resources found in and around the area. With access to some of the world's freshest seafood, chefs and home cooks alike take pride in using locally sourced ingredients to highlight the quality and flavor of their dishes.

Seafood: Homer's position as the "Halibut Capital of the World" ensures that halibut is featured extensively on local menus, served in ways that highlight its fresh, delicate flavor. Salmon, another Alaskan staple, is relished in a variety of ways, including smoked and grilled. The chilly seas also supply abundant seafood, such as oysters, clams, and mussels.

Local Produce: Despite Alaska's hard-growing circumstances, Homer offers an impressive variety of local produce because of its dedicated farming community. During the short but vigorous growing season, local markets are brimming with vivid vegetables and fruits, improving the freshness of culinary choices.

Wild Ingredients: Homer's culinary situation heavily relies on foraging. Local chefs and locals harvest wild berries, mushrooms, and herbs to provide a distinct and authentic Alaskan flavor to their cuisine.

Signature Dishes

Halibut Tacos: Halibut tacos are a simple but wonderful delicacy. These are served at various restaurants along the Homer Spit, where the seafood is exceptionally fresh.

Salmon Berry Jam: This local delicacy embodies the essence of Alaska's environment. Salmon berry jam, made from wild berries in the area, is a delicious delight with a hint of acidity that would be ideal as a gift or for breakfast.

King Crab Legs: Served steaming hot with melted butter, king crab legs are a sumptuous pleasure. These are best savored at one of Homer's superb eating venues overlooking the bay.

Celebrated Restaurants and Eateries

The Mermaid Café: Located on the Homer Spit, this tiny café provides breathtaking views of the mountains and ocean. The café is well-known for its inventive use of local products, and its dishes are both original and comforting.

Captain Pattie's Fish House: Known for its fresh fish, Captain Pattie's is popular with both locals and visitors. The beer-battered halibut is the restaurant's signature dish, a crunchy treat that keeps customers coming back.

Fresh Sourdough Express: This bakery and café promotes sustainability and good eating. It serves everything from hearty soups to freshly baked sourdough bread, all of which are made using organic and locally sourced ingredients.

Food festivals and culinary events

The Homer Halibut Festival is a weekend-long celebration of Homer's most famous fish, featuring fishing competitions, cooking demos, and, of course, lots of halibut dishes to try.

Homer Halibut Festival: The Kachemak Bay Shorebird Festival is largely a birding event, but it also includes local food vendors providing regional specialties, allowing bird enthusiasts to experience local flavors while viewing migratory patterns.

Peony Celebration Day: This celebration, which coincides with the bloom of Homer's gorgeous peonies, also honors the culinary arts, with local chefs serving unique dishes featuring edible flowers and fresh, seasonal foods.

A thriving local brewing and winery scene.

Homer Brewing Company: A pioneer in Homer's craft beer sector, this brewery produces a variety of beers using conventional methods. The Ocean Drive Stout's rich, full-bodied flavor pays homage to Alaska's harsh coastline.

Bear Creek Winery: Bear Creek Winery specializes in fruit wines created from local berries and provides tastings and excursions. Their raspberry dessert wine is a delightful way to conclude any dinner.

Homer's culinary scene is a vibrant and important element of its cultural character, providing insight into the community's relationship to the land and sea. Whether you're eating fresh halibut by the seaside, sipping locally brewed ale, or enjoying a berry dessert prepared with foraged ingredients, Homer's flavors provide a strong feeling of location. This culinary trip not only delights the senses, but also tells the narrative of Homer's environment, people, and traditions.

Family Friendly Guide to Homer, Alaska

Homer, Alaska, known for its magnificent surroundings and dynamic community, also shines as a destination for family-friendly excursions. From engaging activities for children of all ages to educational sites where fun meets learning, Homer provides several chances for families to explore, learn, and make lifelong experiences together. This book explores the many activities and sites in Homer that are ideal for a family outing.

Activities for Children and Families

Beach Exploration at Bishops Beach: Bishop's Beach is one of Homer's most easily accessible and family-friendly destinations. Families can spend the day searching the vast shoreline for intriguing rocks, shells, and tidepool critters. The neighboring Islands and Ocean Visitor Centre frequently organize guided beach walks, during which children can learn about local marine species from trained naturalists.

Horseback Riding Tours: Exploring the picturesque trails of Homer on horseback is a wonderful experience for both children and adults. Local stables provide family-friendly trips for both beginners and seasoned riders. These tours offer a unique viewpoint of Homer's stunning surroundings, including lush woods and panoramic vistas of Kachemak Bay.

Fishing Adventures: Fishing is a traditional Alaskan pastime, and in Homer, even young fisherman can try their luck. Many charter boats are designed to accommodate families and have all the required equipment. Fishing, whether for halibut or salmon, can be an exciting and gratifying pastime, especially when the entire family joins in.

Kayaking and paddleboarding: For families who enjoy water sports, kayaking and paddleboarding in Kachemak Bay's protected waters provide a safe and enjoyable way to explore. Several local outfitters sell gear for kids and beginners, and guided trips provide a safe atmosphere for all family members to explore the bay's beauty up close.

Family Workshops at the Bunnell Street Arts Centre: The Bunnell Street Arts Centre caters not only to adult artists but also to families and children through workshops and classes. These activities range from pottery-making to painting, giving youngsters a creative outlet while also teaching them about local art and culture.

Educational Spots

Pratt Museum: The Pratt Museum houses a wealth of information on local history and natural science. The museum's displays range from marine life to Alaskan homesteading, making it an engaging learning setting for children. Interactive displays, such as a reproduction of a seabird colony and a live-feed video of a real bald eagle nest, provide children with hands-on experience with the local ecosystem.

The Alaska Islands and Ocean Visitor Centre: This educational center is a great place to learn about the marine ecology of Kachemak Bay and the Alaska Maritime National Wildlife Refuge. The tourist center has interactive exhibits, a well-designed children's area, and instructional films. It also serves as a starting point for guided nature walks, which allow families to learn about coastal ecology and wildlife.

Wynn Nature Centre: The Wynn Nature Centre, operated by the Centre for Alaskan Coastal Studies, provides family-friendly guided nature tours. Located on 140 acres of meadows and forests, the center offers educational programs on local flora and fauna, emphasizing the significance of conservation. Kids can go on guided treks, scavenger hunts, and animal viewing expeditions.

Seldovia Day Trip: Seldovia, a short ferry journey from Homer, provides a lovely and instructive day trip for families. The Seldovia Village Tribe Natural Resources Department offers tours that teach visitors about the local Indigenous culture and environmental stewardship methods. Families can spend the day exploring the town, visiting the Seldovia Museum, and walking the Otterbahn Trail.

Halibut Cove: Halibut Cove, which can be reached by ferry, is a one-of-a-kind combination of environment and culture. Families can stroll the boardwalks, visit local galleries, and enjoy the peaceful, car-free environment. The Halibut Cove Lagoon includes boardwalks and paths for easy walks suited for young children, giving both educational content and physical activity in a beautiful setting.

Homer, Alaska, offers a distinct blend of outdoor activities and educational possibilities that are great for families seeking both adventure and instruction. Each activity and site provides an opportunity to learn about this magnificent region's rich natural and cultural history. Whether through hands-on inquiry, guided tours, or creative workshops, families visiting Homer can expect an enlightening experience that is both educational and entertaining.

Nature & Wildlife in Homer, Alaska

Homer, Alaska, is a nature and wildlife refuge located on the magnificent Kachemak Bay. This gorgeous location not only provides breathtaking scenery but also acts as a home for a broad range of wildlife species, including majestic bald eagles and elusive sea otters.

Along with its great biodiversity, Homer is dedicated to conservation measures that will preserve its natural beauty for future generations. This guide investigates the local fauna, addresses the need for conservation, and recommends the best places to capture the essence of Homer via photography.

A Guide to Local Wildlife.

Marine life: Homer's proximity to the frigid seas of the North Pacific and Kachemak Bay provide a fertile maritime habitat for a diversified aquatic ecology. Key species are:

Sea Otters: These attractive creatures can often be seen floating on their backs near Homer Spit, cracking open mussels with rocks.

Humpback whales and orcas: These majestic whales can be seen breaching and feeding in the bay during the summer. Whale-watching trips allow guests to witness these massive creatures up close.

Halibut and Salmon: The waters around Homer are loaded with fish, making it an ideal fishing destination. Salmon's life cycle, from spawning to adulthood, is vital to the local ecology, supporting both other wildlife and the local fishing industry.

Terrestrial animals

On land, Homer's forests, meadows, and coastal areas provide habitat for a diverse range of species.

Moose: These enormous mammals are frequently observed in town and the adjacent wilderness areas, particularly at dawn and twilight.

Bald Eagles: Homer is notable for its high bald eagle population. These birds of prey are frequently spotted perched on trees or flying overhead in quest of fish.

Brown and Black Bears: Brown and black bears are less common within city limits, but they can be seen in the more isolated areas surrounding Homer. Observing these powerful creatures necessitates caution and respect for their natural behaviors.

Conservation Efforts

Homer's natural beauty and biodiversity are always under threat from human activity and environmental changes. Recognizing these issues, the community and various organizations have developed several conservation programs.

Habitat Protection: Many species rely on conservation efforts to survive. Organisations such as the Kachemak Bay Research Reserve aim to investigate and protect the region's unique habitats.

Wildlife Rehabilitation: The Alaska Maritime National Wildlife Refuge, in collaboration with local rehabilitation centers, strives to rescue and rehabilitate wounded wildlife, mostly seabirds and marine mammals. These facilities are critical to preserving the population health of these species.

Sustainable practices: Homer promotes sustainable tourism and fishing techniques. Fishing restrictions and rigorous guidelines for wildlife excursions ensure that natural behaviors and habitats are disturbed to the least extent possible. The community also emphasizes recycling and sustainable waste management to help residents and visitors lessen their environmental impact.

Education & Outreach: Education is an important instrument for conservation. Local institutions, such as the Pratt Museum and the Islands and Ocean Visitor Centre, provide educational programs to teach visitors and residents about the need to maintain Homer's natural resources.

Photography Spots

For photographers, Homer offers a plethora of great locations to capture the diverse landscapes and lively wildlife:

Beluga Point: Beluga Point, with its sweeping views of Kachemak Bay, is an ideal spot for landscape and wildlife photography. Photographers frequently get photographs of feeding birds, frolicking sea otters, and the occasional whale.

Homer spits: This long, narrow landform extends into the bay, offering panoramic views of the surrounding mountains and ocean. The Spit is also an excellent location to shoot bald eagles and other seabirds.

Skyline Drive Overlook: Skyline Drive offers a spectacular view of Homer and the surrounding mountains and lakes. Sunrise and sunset are especially lovely periods for photographers.

Grewingk Glacier Lake: This glacier-fed lake is surrounded by towering mountains and lush forests and may be reached by hiking or boat taxi. It's the best location for photographing spectacular landscapes and reflections.

Wynn Nature Centre: This 140-acre refuge is ideal for capturing wildflowers, deep woodlands, and wildlife like moose and bears in their natural environment.

Homer, Alaska, is a veritable treasure trove of natural beauties and wildlife, with infinite chances for adventure, conservation, and photography. Visitors and residents may help to keep Homer a pristine wilderness for future generations by respecting and safeguarding its distinctive environments. Whether you're witnessing its diverse marine life, hiking through lush terrain, or photographing its splendor, Homer invites you to connect directly with nature.

Day Trips and Excursions from Homer, Alaska

Homer, Alaska, frequently referred to as the doorway to adventure, has a variety of day outings and excursions that promise stunning views and personal encounters with nature. Whether exploring the tranquil town of Seldovia, traveling across Kachemak Bay, or going on an exciting bear sighting tour, Homer's accessibility to different landscapes and wildlife habitats makes it a great base for exploring Alaska's outdoors. This guide takes an in-depth look at some of the most exciting day trips and excursions available in Homer.

Seldovia: A Relaxing Escape

Seldovia, located on the south side of Kachemak Bay, is a lovely village that takes you back in time to a simpler, more relaxed way of life. This lovely village, only reachable by boat or plane, is well-known for its breathtaking beauty, rich history, and welcoming residents.

Activities and attractions in Seldovia

Take a stroll down Seldovia's historic Main Street, which is lined with a wooden boardwalk. The road is lined with quaint boutiques, art galleries, and cozy cafes that provide an insight into the town's history and present.

Otterbahn walk: A popular nature walk that travels through thick woodlands to a stunning beach, with opportunities for wildlife observations and spectacular vistas.

Kayaking and paddleboarding: Seldovia's protected waters are ideal for these activities. Visitors may explore the shoreline at their leisure thanks to rental options and guided trips.

Seldovia Village Tribe Cultural Centre: Discover the rich traditions of the indigenous Dena'ina and Sugpiaq peoples who have lived here for generations. The center provides exhibits and cultural demonstrations that help visitors understand the area's history.

Getting To Seldovia: The trip to Seldovia is part of the adventure. Ferries and water taxis depart from Homer regularly, offering spectacular views of Kachemak Bay along the way. Alternatively, small planes provide fast flights with a bird's-eye perspective of the stunning countryside below.

Kachemak Bay

Kachemak Bay State Park and its surrounding wilderness provide some of Alaska's most accessible and breathtaking natural beauty. The area is ideal for outdoor enthusiasts, with activities suitable for all ages and abilities.

Activities Across the Bay:

Hiking: Trails such as the Glacier Lake Trail and Grewingk Glacier Spit provide varying levels of difficulty while rewarding hikers with breathtaking views of glaciers, mountains, and the ocean.

Boating and Fishing: Reserve a boat for a day of fishing or scenic cruising. Halibut, salmon, and other marine species thrive in Kachemak Bay's rich waters.

Wildlife Tours: Guided tours allow you to see sea otters, seals, porpoises, and a variety of seabirds up close. These tours emphasize the bay's ecological diversity and provide insights into local marine life.

Plan Your Trip: When planning a day trip across the bay, keep in mind that the tides and weather conditions can change dramatically. Local tour operators are invaluable resources for making the most of your visit, as they provide expertise and equipment to ensure a safe and enjoyable experience.

Bear Viewing Excursions

The Thrill of Seeing Alaskan Bears: A bear-viewing trip is one of Homer's most thrilling excursions. These excursions typically take visitors to either Katmai National Park or Lake Clark National Park, where brown bears are often seen in their natural habitats.

What to Expect on a Bear Viewing Trip:

Flightseeing Adventure: Most bear-viewing tours begin with a scenic flight on a small plane, offering dramatic views of the volcanoes, mountains, and wilderness of the Alaska Peninsula.

Guided Viewing: Upon landing, experienced guides lead visitors to safe viewing areas where they can observe bears fishing for salmon, playing, or lounging on the beach.

Photography Opportunities: These excursions provide unparalleled opportunities for wildlife photography. Guides often offer tips for capturing stunning photos while maintaining a safe distance from the animals.

Safety and Ethics: Safety is paramount on bear viewing excursions. Guides are trained to keep visitors safe and to minimize the impact on the wildlife. Following their instructions is essential for a safe and respectful experience.

Day trips and excursions from Homer offer a diverse range of experiences that allow visitors to immerse themselves in the natural beauty and unique cultures of Alaska. Whether you choose a peaceful day in

Seldovia, an adventurous excursion across Kachemak Bay, or a thrilling bear-viewing adventure, each experience promises to enrich your understanding and appreciation of this spectacular region. These excursions not only highlight the ecological and cultural richness of Alaska but also foster a deeper connection with the natural world, leaving lasting memories that beckon travelers back to Homer time and again.

Shopping and Souvenirs in Homer, Alaska

Homer, Alaska, a gorgeous village nestled on the shore of Kachemak Bay, is not only a destination for adventurers and nature lovers but also a thriving center for shopping and local crafts. The town offers a unique shopping experience, distinguished by a vast selection of local products that represent the cultural legacy and natural beauty of the region.

This detailed guide will show you through the best places to buy in Homer, highlight distinctive local items and crafts, and provide recommendations for ethical shopping, ensuring that your purchases contribute positively to the community and environment.

Best Places to Shop in Homer

Old Inlet Bookshop: For those who value the written word, Old Inlet Bookshop is a treasure mine of new, used, and rare books. Nestled in the heart of Homer, this charming bookstore encourages you to browse its large collection, which includes works by Alaskan authors and volumes on local history and animals. It's the perfect spot to find a keepsake that captures the essence of Alaska.

Homer Farmers Market: Operating from May through September, the Homer Farmers Market is a must-visit for anybody wishing to immerse themselves in local culture. Here, you may purchase fresh vegetables, handmade crafts, and unique gourmet products directly from local growers and artists. The market not only supports the local economy but also offers things that are fresh, sustainable, and distinctive to the region.

Bunnell Street Arts Center: This arts facility is more than simply a gallery; it's a communal hub where local artists sell their work. From exquisite pottery and sculptures to fine art and handcrafted jewelry, each piece available here is unique. Bunnell not only sells one-of-a-kind souvenirs, but it also promotes the local artistic community.

Nomar: If you want something practical yet authentically Alaskan, Nomar's shop on Pioneer Avenue is the place to go. Nomar is well-known for producing high-quality outdoor clothing that is customized to the Alaskan lifestyle, such as the famed "Homer Spit Pullover." These items are fantastic gifts for those who value durability and style.

Alaska Wild Berry Products: No trip to Homer is complete without trying or buying some local berry products. Alaska Wild Berry Products sells a delicious selection of jams, jellies, and chocolates created from Alaskan berries. Their store is an excellent place to find sweet delights that evoke the flavors of the surrounding environment.

Unique Local Products and Crafts

Ulu Knifes: The ulu knife is one of Alaska's most distinctive items of handicraft. These curved knives, which have traditionally been used by Alaska's Indigenous peoples, are extremely versatile and can be used to cut anything from vegetables to meat and fish. Local artists frequently work with local materials like caribou antlers to make them both utilitarian and beautiful.

Qviut Products: Qiviut, the muskox's underwool, is known to be lighter and warmer than sheep wool. Local artists spin the fiber into yarn, which they then weave into hats, scarves, and mittens. These products are not only exquisite but also extremely warm and soft, ideal for cold Alaskan evenings.

Birch Syrup: While maple syrup has gained popularity, birch syrup is a unique Alaskan product with a nuanced, rich flavor character that ranges from savory to sweet. In the spring, local producers tap birch trees to extract sap, which is then converted into syrup. This wonderful product is a must-try and makes an excellent present or souvenir.

Tips For Ethical Shopping

Support Local Artists and Craftsmen: When shopping in Homer, prioritize shops that feature local artists and craftspeople. This not only supports the local economy but also fosters a dynamic cultural community. Purchasing directly from the creators guarantees that they are fairly compensated for their efforts.

Eco-friendly products: Choose sustainable products, particularly when purchasing items common to the region such as fish, fur, or wood products. Look for certificates or inquire with store owners about the sources of their products to guarantee that your purchases are environmentally responsible.

Cultural sensitivity: When shopping for things, keep cultural heritage in mind, especially if they feature native designs or processes. It is critical to respect and honor Indigenous peoples' customs and heritage by ensuring that these artifacts are sustainably sourced and that the proceeds assist the right communities.

Avoid Over-Touristed Items: While it may be tempting to buy mass-produced mementos, consider the consequences of your purchasing selections.

Choose things created locally that do not contribute to environmental deterioration or cultural dilution.

Shopping in Homer provides a unique opportunity to discover and interact with the local culture with its diverse selection of items and crafts. Visitors can enjoy their vacations while also supporting local businesses by shopping responsibly. Whether it's the intricate workmanship of an ulu knife, the warmth of qiviut wool, or the distinct flavor of birch syrup, the treasures found in Homer will leave you with long-lasting memories of your Alaska experience.

Nightlife & Entertainment in Homer, Alaska

Homer, Alaska, is well-known for its beautiful daylight beauty and animals, but its evening and entertainment offers are equally appealing. As the sun sets over Kachemak Bay, the city comes alive with a diverse range of alternatives to suit all interests and ages.

From cozy bars and bustling clubs to exciting live music and performances, Homer provides one-of-a-kind nighttime activities to make your Alaskan nights memorable. This detailed guide explores Homer's greatest nightlife and entertainment establishments, highlighting where to go and what to do when twilight falls over this gorgeous town.

Bars and Clubs

The Salty Dog Saloon: The Salty Dawg Saloon, located on the famed Homer Spit, is a must-see destination for any visitor. This tavern, housed in a historic structure dating back to 1897, exudes character and charm, as proven by its walls plastered in dollar notes from customers all around the globe. It is known for its welcoming environment and distinctive décor, as well as its selection of local beers and spirits. It's the ideal venue to meet residents and visitors alike.

Alice's Champagne Palace: Alice's Champagne Palace is a Homer institution that serves a wide variety of cocktails and features live entertainment. Alice's is the perfect place to unwind with a specialty drink or a local brew, thanks to its big layout and warm, inviting vibe. The venue routinely provides live music and quiz evenings, making it an exciting place to spend an evening.

DownEast Saloon: The Down East Saloon, located just outside of downtown Homer, provides an authentic Alaskan bar experience with its rustic surroundings and eclectic event calendar. This establishment offers karaoke nights, live bands, and outside activities such as horseshoes and a fire pit.

It's a terrific place to soak in Homer's local flavor while having a relaxed and enjoyable evening.

Live Music and Performance

The Bunnell Street Arts Centre: As a cultural hub in Homer, the Bunnell Street Arts Centre not only exhibits visual arts but also hosts live concerts. From local singer-songwriters to traveling bands and performance artists, the center hosts a diverse spectrum of musical and creative performances. Attending a performance here allows you to experience Homer's creative heart.

Homer Council for the Arts: The Homer Council on the Arts is instrumental in presenting varied acts to the community, including classical music concerts, jazz nights, dramatic theatre, and dance performances. Their event calendar is jam-packed with cultural activities that entertain while also expanding visitors' appreciation of Alaska's artistic legacy.

Mariner Theatre at Homer High School: The Mariner Theatre at Homer High School is a popular venue for larger productions such as concerts, plays, and dance performances. This theatre frequently organizes programs that appeal to a wide range of people, making it a staple of community entertainment and a meeting place for those who like the performing arts.

Evening Activities for All Ages

Movies at Homer Theatre: For a more leisurely evening, the Homer Theatre, the Kenai Peninsula's first and only digital 3D and Surround Sound theatre shows a wide range of films, including blockbusters, indies, and documentaries. It is a family-friendly establishment that periodically hosts special events such as film festivals and movie marathons.

Educational talks and nighttime walks: Several organizations in Homer, notably the Alaska Maritime National Wildlife Refuge and the Centre for Alaskan Coastal Studies, provide evening seminars and guided nocturnal nature hikes. These activities are ideal for families and anyone looking to learn more about Alaska's natural surroundings and animals. They offer an exceptional opportunity to explore Homer's landscapes in the ethereal glow of twilight.

Bowling in Kachemak Bowl: Kachemak Bowl is the go-to place for family amusement in the evening. Whether you're a seasoned bowler or simply looking for a fun night out with the family, Kachemak Bowl provides a welcoming environment with various lanes and other games to ensure everyone has a good time.

Homer's nightlife and entertainment scene has something for everyone. From the rustic appeal of local taverns and the cultural depth of live performances to family-friendly activities like films and bowling, the town ensures that your Alaskan nights are as fascinating as your days. Each place and activity described not only adds fun and enjoyment to your vacation but also allows you to experience

Homer's community spirit and cultural energy after dark. Whether you're clinking drinks at the Salty Dawg Saloon, cheering on a live performance at the Bunnell Street Arts Centre, or learning about local animals on a twilight stroll, Homer guarantees an amazing evening beneath the huge Alaskan sky.

Practical Tips for Visitors to Homer, Alaska

When visiting Homer, Alaska, it is critical to be well-prepared with useful information to guarantee a safe and pleasurable vacation. This comprehensive guide covers everything from where to get emergency assistance to understanding banking alternatives and how to stay connected. Whether you're planning a long stay or a short visit, knowing about these details will help you navigate your vacation more quickly and efficiently.

Emergency Contacts and Healthcare

Emergency services: 911 is the universal emergency number in the United States for obtaining quick assistance in the event of a fire, medical emergency, or a crime.

Homer Volunteer Fire Department: Located on Heath Street, they offer both fire and emergency medical services.

The Homer Police Department is located on Heath Street, near the fire department, and provides police assistance.

Healthcare Facilities: South Peninsula Hospital is Homer's major hospital, providing extensive medical services like emergency care, inpatient and outpatient treatments, and specialized clinics. It is located on Bartlett Street and is well-equipped to meet a wide range of medical needs.

Homer Medical Centre is a family medical clinic that provides preventative care, check-ups, and treatment for a variety of medical ailments.

In addition, Homer has several private clinics and dental offices that provide anything from routine check-ups to specialized medical care.

Pharmacies

Ulmer's Drug and Hardware: Located on Lake Street, this store has a pharmacy and offers prescription and over-the-counter pharmaceuticals.

Safeway Pharmacy: Located within the Safeway supermarket on Greatland Street and provides a comprehensive variety of pharmaceutical services.

Banking & Currency Exchange

Local banking:

First National Bank Alaska: As one of Alaska's leading banks, it operates branches and ATMs in Homer. This bank provides full banking services, such as account opening, loans, and more.

Alaska USA Federal Credit Union: Another banking choice that offers similar services in the comfort of a nearby location.

Currency Exchange:

Banks: Most banks in Homer can exchange foreign money, however, it's best to check ahead of time to see if they have the currency you're looking for or if there is a waiting period.

Anchorage International Airport: For international visitors, exchanging cash at the Anchorage

International Airport upon arrival in Alaska may be the most expedient choice before traveling to Homer.

ATMs: Homer has various ATMs that are strategically placed in locations such as banks, grocery stores, and downtown districts. These machines accept all major credit and debit cards, making it easy to withdraw cash at any time.

Connectivity: Internet and Phone Services.

Internet services:

Home Internet Providers: GCI and Alaska Communications offer high-speed internet to Homer residents and businesses. They provide numerous options based on speed and data requirements.

Wi-Fi Hotspots: Many public sites offer free Wi-Fi, including the Homer Public Library, coffee shops, and certain restaurants. The Homer Spit, a famous tourist destination, also includes areas with free Wi-Fi connections.

Telephone Services:

Mobile Network Providers: Major US providers such as AT&T, Verizon, and T-Mobile provide decent coverage in Homer, particularly downtown and along major routes. However, coverage can be patchy in distant places or along hiking paths.

International Visitors: If you're traveling from abroad, you should check with your service provider about international roaming rates or consider acquiring a local SIM card for the duration of your stay.

Tips For Staying Connected

Planning Ahead: If you expect to need reliable internet for business or extensive phone use, investigate choices such as portable Wi-Fi routers or plans with substantial data allotment.

Communication Apps: Using apps such as WhatsApp, Skype, or FaceTime can help you stay in touch with friends and family without incurring high phone bills, especially for overseas visitors.

Understanding and accessing practical information such as emergency contacts, health care services, banking, and connectivity alternatives is critical for anybody visiting Homer, Alaska. Being prepared in these areas not only makes for a safer and more pleasant vacation but also improves your whole experience in this picturesque and hospitable town. Whether you require medical support, financial services, or simply want to keep connected, Homer has everything you need.

Conclusion: Departing Thoughts

As your journey in Homer, Alaska, comes to an end, take some time to reflect on the events and memories you've made. This ruggedly gorgeous and culturally rich corner of the earth is more than simply a tourist attraction; it is an immersion adventure into an environment where nature and mankind coexist harmoniously. This final chapter is more than just a farewell; it is an invitation to carry Homer's spirit with you, an encouragement to let the teachings and beauty of this special location resonate in your daily life.

Homer has most certainly imprinted on your mind magnificent views of sprawling mountains descending into a bright sea, where eagles fly high and whales break the waters of Kachemak Bay. Perhaps you hiked through lush paths, paddled along quiet seas, or watched the fiery kiss of the sun lowering into the ocean. These natural beauties are not only breathtaking, but they also serve as emotional reminders of the Earth's beauty and the importance of protecting such resources. Homer, with its extensive wilderness and dedicated conservation initiatives, teaches the value of stewardship—being caretakers of the world we inhabit.

Every location, street, and face in Homer's world has a tale. Homer is a tapestry of history and creativity, from the fascinating local artists who capture Alaska's soul in brilliant colors and textures to the indigenous tradition that runs through the country. You may remember the warmth of a grin in a crowded market, the stories told in a cozy gallery, or the hearty laughter shared over a delicious seafood lunch. These cultural encounters enrich the tourist experience by providing a deeper knowledge of the different fabric that comprises the Homer community.

Travel has a significant impact on human development, and a trip to Homer is no exception. Perhaps you discovered a new interest in wildlife photography, experienced the excitement of catching (and releasing) a wild salmon, or felt the calm satisfaction of reaching the top of a difficult trek. Perhaps you learned the virtues of simplicity and sustainability from the way Homerites lived in harmony with the land and sea. These encounters shape attitudes and priorities, frequently resulting in a renewed respect for nature and a commitment to an environmentally sustainable lifestyle.

If Homer has touched your heart, it could be because of the connections he has made with other people and the environment. You may leave with friendships that can be carried across long distances, as well as promises of returns or reunion. Visitors leave feeling like honorary locals rather than tourists, thanks to the community's warm demeanor. These links enhance our global village, reminding us of our common obligations and joys.

As you leave Homer, consider how you can take a bit of it with you. Perhaps it's by promoting sustainability in your town, fighting for wildlife conservation, or supporting local artists and small businesses. Each souvenir, photo, and memory has the potential to be a catalyst for positive change and an ambassador for Homer's values of cultural and environmental preservation.

Your voyage to Homer may come to an end, but the story you've created there will live on. The stories you tell, the behaviors you follow, and the awareness you raise will have an impact on others and integrate the essence of Homer into larger conversations and activities. Homer's horizon is more than just a barrier where the sea meets the sky; it is a continuous line that encourages you to go beyond, to learn endlessly, and to behave carefully.

When you leave Homer, you carry on the legacy of a place where each wave, pebble, and breeze tells a narrative about the earth's beauty and tenacity. May your journeys away from Homer be safe and introspective, and may your return be as certain as the tides that caress its beaches. Remember that each farewell is a pause in the endless adventure that awaits in Homer, Alaska.

Appendix

Useful Apps

Alaska Traveler Information - Provides real-time travel advisories and road conditions.

MyRadar - Weather app that provides local weather forecasts and live radar maps.

Audubon Bird Guide - A must-have for bird watchers visiting Homer, with detailed information and sounds.

Tides Near Me - Offers real-time tide information, crucial for beach walks and fishing in Homer.

AllTrails - Lists detailed hiking trails around Homer, including user reviews and trail difficulty ratings.

Emergency Contacts

Emergency Services (Police, Fire, Medical): Dial 911

South Peninsula Hospital:

Address: 4300 Bartlett Street, Homer, AK 99603

Phone: +1 907-235-8101

Homer Police Department:

Address: 4060 Heath Street, Homer, AK 99603

Phone: +1 907-235-3150

Homer Volunteer Fire Department:

Address: 604 E Pioneer Ave, Homer, AK 99603

Phone: +1 907-235-3155

Frequently Asked Questions (FAQs)

What is the best time to visit Homer, Alaska?

- The best time to visit Homer is during the summer months from June to August when the weather is mild, and the days are long, offering ample opportunities for wildlife viewing and outdoor activities.

Are there any activities for children in Homer?

- Yes, Homer offers several family-friendly activities, including beach exploration, interactive programs at the Alaska Islands and Ocean Visitor Center, and nature trails suitable for children at Carl Wynn Nature Center.

How do I get around in Homer?

- Renting a car is the most convenient way to explore Homer and its surroundings extensively. However, there are also taxis and bike rentals available for shorter distances or specific tours.

What are some must-try local foods?

- Don't miss out on fresh halibut, king crab, and salmon dishes. For a unique local treat, try the reindeer sausage and birch syrup products.

What should I bring for a trip to Homer?

- Pack layers including a waterproof jacket, as weather can be unpredictable. Also, bring binoculars for bird watching, a good camera, sunblock, mosquito repellent, and sturdy walking or hiking shoes.

Travel Checklist

- Clothing for variable weather (layers, rain gear)
- Comfortable walking/hiking shoes
- Sunscreen and sunglasses
- Insect repellent
- Camera with extra batteries
- Binoculars for wildlife and bird watching
- Personal medications and first aid kit
- Refillable water bottle
- Daypack for excursions

Travel Itineraries

3-Day Itinerary

Day 1: Explore the Homer Spit; visit the Pratt Museum and the Islands and Ocean Visitor Center. Dinner at a local seafood restaurant.

Day 2: Take a wildlife and glacier tour of Kachemak Bay; picnic lunch on a secluded beach. Evening at Salty Dawg Saloon.

Day 3: Hike the trails at Wynn Nature Center. Shop for souvenirs at local galleries and boutiques.

5-Day Itinerary

Day 1-3: Follow the 3-day itinerary.

Day 4: Day trip to Seldovia with exploration of the historic boardwalk and art galleries. Kayaking in the afternoon.

Day 5: Attend a workshop at Bunnell Street Arts Center. Evening stroll on Bishop's Beach and casual dining downtown.

7-Day Itinerary

Day 1-5: Follow the 5-day itinerary.

Day 6: Bear viewing excursion to Katmai or Lake Clark National Park.

Day 7: Spend a leisurely day exploring local cafes and the Homer Farmers Market. Finish with a scenic drive along Skyline Drive for panoramic views.

Made in the USA
Coppell, TX
06 August 2024

35649595R00075